READ THIS FIRST

We are educating
the next generation of risk-takers.
Grab our Risk-Taking Tips for
Leaders Newsletter NOW!
Sign up at
bit.ly/RiskTakingTipsForLeaders

FLIP THIS RISK® FOR PODCASTING

TOP RISKS EVERY PODCASTER SHOULD AVOID TO BE SUCCESSFUL

KAREN HARDY

62 Media Publishing

Published in the United States of America by 62 Media Publishing, Upper Marlboro, Maryland

ISBN: 978-1-7358786-2-1

Book Interior and Ebook Design by Amit Dey

Definition

1. Flip This Risk® (verb). The act of turning the odds against you in your favor.

What People Are Saying About Flip This Risk®

Dr. Karen Hardy is born for this job! She is knowledgeable, super-smart, and yet has the human warmth to bring out the best in her guests.

—Mitzi Perdue (Mrs. Frank Perdue),
co-author of How to Be Up in Down Times

I think the Flip This Risk® podcasts will open the eyes of many executives. I like your broad approach towards risk. Interviewing a wide variety of people in different roles of taking and managing risks is the best way to go.

—Kristina Narvaez,
co-author Strategic Risk Management:
New Tools for Competitive
Advantage in an Uncertain Age

To anyone interested in risk management, I highly recommend tuning in to Dr. Karen Hardy's podcast series, Flip This Risk®. She interviews influential leaders to get their thoughts on risk management.

—Chris Bloxham

Dr. Karen Hardy is a magnificent podcaster. She loves doing enlightening, exciting, and challenging interviews to overcome everyone's aversion to risk. I predict she will help millions break free of the crippling fears of RISK!

—Mark Victor Hansen,
co-creator of the Chicken Soup for the Soul series

Dr. Hardy continues to provide relevant and valuable information on her platform that touches all communities. I have a more informed perspective on risk and incorporating risk-mitigating strategies in my life. Thank you!

—B. Adkins

Dr. Karen Hardy cares about her listeners. She cares about giving them value and hope.

—Dr. Mark Goulston,
host of My WakeUp Call podcast

Dr. Hardy has a lot of excellent information that can serve a lot of people.

—Sean Briscombe,
CEO of The Kind Foundation

Flip This Risk is a creative and intelligent podcast that can help challenge, encourage, and inspire your growth.

—J. Isaacson, Freelance Writer,
Project Magazine Online

Dr. Karen Hardy has a remarkable podcast, and if you have not tuned in check, it out! An insightful resource for anyone interested in learning more about the risk management industry as well.

—Lalia L.

Contents

Introduction

In a small focus group open to the LinkedIn community, members were asked in an informal, voluntary survey about their relationship with risk-taking.

Sixty-five percent of those who participated said they have no problem taking risks, while 34 percent said they were hesitant about Risk-taking and needed to take more risks.

Extrapolated over a population, we can assume that this perceived fear of risk-taking could be a stumbling block for millions of people—in their professional, business, and personal endeavors! I also spent time pitching the idea of risk management to communities not involved in the risk management profession— people in the arts, entertainment, and other local groups, and gathered feedback about their perceptions of risk management. Again, many did not see the connection of risk

"We have learned that RISK is not only the effect of uncertainty on our business objectives; but is also the effect of uncertainty on our personal objectives."

management to their lives or their work.

Once I gathered this additional input, I set out to find answers to this problem by asking thought leaders and action takers **this one specific question** to help improve the mindset of millions about risk:

What is the relationship high achievers have with risk taking and how does it influence their leadership abilities?

In my more than fifteen years in the risk management profession, leading initiatives and consulting with organizations, I discovered that the everyday person does not relate to or fully understand the technical but powerful risk management practices.

During the pandemic, many hardworking people panicked about the uncertainty we faced.

While organizations sought the expertise and advice of professional risk practitioners, mom-and-pop stores and other small businesses did not have immediate access to this critical business skill set. Research shows that we can train our brains to react to a crisis less emotionally and more rationally. Scholars also discovered that pre-crisis training could make a difference. Imagine if everyone was pre-trained on dealing with the unknown—or uncertainty before the pandemic hit? We may not stop negative things from happening, but we can learn how to navigate through them to find the positive side of it. We can learn how to build up these risk management skills within ourselves and then use them to achieve business and personal success.

The combination of these revelations caused me to believe that it is time for a change!

We are helping millions break free of their crippling fears of risk and uncertainty!

I believe it is time for a new conversation and awareness about risk management that invites everyone to the table *from the boardroom to the barber down the street!*

And it all starts with Flip This Risk® branded books.

HOW TO USE THIS BOOK

Simplicity is the ultimate sophistication

— Leonardo da Vinci

As a risk management professional, I have found that there is one thing to be true over the years: The simpler, the better.

All too often, we assume that the more technical terms we use to convey a message, the more effective we are. That cannot be further from reality.

The message of this book is that we all need to apply risk management skills to be successful in life and business—including podcasters!

The message of this book is that we all need to apply risk management skills to be successful in life and in business—including podcasters!

The Merriam-Webster dictionary defines **opportunity** as "a favorable juncture of circumstances; a good chance for advancement and progress."

This book is for those excited about pursuing current market opportunities in podcasting but unaware of the valuable skill risk management plays in attaining great success.

For nearly a decade, I physically walked the hallways of a 1.8 million-square-foot building, knocking on doors to make my pitch to leaders about the importance of risk management. From those early experiences, I learned the value of **simplicity**—in conversations and communications when it came to sharing complex ideas.

That experience has inspired this book!

The goal is to make the topic of risk management conversational and relatable through the stories and experiences of real people—bypassing the stuffy corporate lingo.

We created a conversational book format. It can spark positive conversations and even healthy debates around the best practices for managing Risk.

Based on my career observations, I have crafted **Flip This Risk® for Podcasting: Top Risks Every Podcaster Should Avoid to be Successful.**

The intent is simple: I want to get you ready for success and make sure it sticks!

This book includes exercises for practicing how to assess the risks associated with podcasting. It includes interviews with some of the top podcasters and tips to help you avoid the pitfalls.

Podcasting is a lucrative opportunity. Armed with the right risk management skills and knowledge, you can reap great rewards and benefits. **-FTR BOOKS**

1

A Little History Never Hurts

Have you ever invested in bitcoin or cryptocurrency without researching the industry first? Probably not!

Most people who jump into a career or serious hobby can benefit from a vested interest in the history of that area. The same goes for podcasting as well.

Technically speaking, a **"Podcast"** is a combination of "iPod" and broadcast." The term "podcasting" was first suggested by *The Guardian* columnist and BBC journalist Ben Hammersley, who invented it in early February 2004 while writing an article for *The Guardian.*

The term was first used in the audio-blogging community in September 2004, when Danny Gregoire introduced it in a message to the iPodder-dev mailing list, from

> **"Consider the purpose of the podcast. What are you trying to share, teach, or explain?"**
>
> **- Flip This Risk® Books**

where it was adopted by Adam Curry.

The content can be accessed using any computer or similar device that can play media files. Use of the term "podcast" predated Apple's addition of formal support for podcasting to the iPod, or its iTunes software. Other names for podcasting include "netcast," intended as a vendor-neutral term without the loose reference to the Apple iPod. This name is used by shows from the TWiT.tv network. Some sources have also suggested the backronym "portable on-demand" or "POD" for similar reasons.

The verb "subscribe" has often been used to denote the process of receiving podcasts. By 2021, as the term could be implanted to suggest that obtaining a podcast required a paid subscription, Apple, Amazon, Audible, Spotify, and Stitcher had shifted to using the verb "fol-low" to align themselves with terminology commonly used social networking services.

In October 2000, the concept of attaching sound and video files in RSS feeds was proposed in a draft by Tristan

Louis. The idea was implemented by Dave Winer, a software developer and an author of the RSS format.

Podcasting, once an obscure method of spreading audio information, has become a recognized medium for distributing audio content, whether for corporate or personal use.

Podcasts are similar to radio programs in form, but they exist as audio files that can be played at a listener›s convenience, anytime or anywhere.

NOTES

2

What is a Podcast?

A **podcast** is an episodic series of spoken word digital audio files that users can download to a personal device for easy listening. Streaming applications and podcasting services provide a convenient and integrated way to manage a personal consumption queue across many podcast sources and playback devices.

A podcast series usually features one or more recurring hosts engaged in discussing a particular topic or current event. Discussion and content within a podcast can range from carefully scripted to entirely improvised.

Podcasts combine elaborate and artistic sound production with thematic concerns ranging from scientific research to slice-of-life journalism.

Many podcast series provides an associated website with links and show notes, guest biographies, transcripts, additional resources, commentary, and even a community forum dedicated to discussing the show's content.

> **"Podcasters... have an ability to build an intimate relationship with their listeners that they can also leverage to grow their business..."**
>
> **— Corey Poirier**

The cost to the consumer is low.

While many podcasts are free to download, some are underwritten by corporations or sponsored, including commercial advertisements.

In other cases, a podcast could also be a business venture supported by some combination of a paid subscription model, advertising, or product delivered after sale.

Why Do People Start Podcasts?

People are motivated to create a podcast for several reasons:

20% of adults report listening to podcasts at least occasionally. That's a lot of people you can reach with your voice!

Podcasting is much less crowded than blogging. The blogging landscape is very crowded.

The podcast producer, who is often the podcast host as well, may wish to express a personal passion, increase professional visibility, enter a social network of influencers or influential ideas, or cultivate a community of like-minded viewership.

People can do other things while they listen.

Think of all the activities that can be performed while listening to a podcast:

- Work out
- Take a walk
- Drive
- Sit by the pool

With a podcast, listeners can experience more intimacy. The written word is no substitute for the spoken word. With a podcast, you can connect on a whole new level. You can reach a new crowd. Many people may not read a blog but will listen to a podcast.

Podcasting also has many advantages over other forms of online marketing. You can provide value in a new and more meaningful way. Podcasting is even easier than blogging because you do not need a website to get started.

Why do you want to start a podcast?

NOTES

3

How to Produce a Podcast

So, are you ready to get to work? This information is an introductory podcast 101 for some. It is perfect if you are new to podcasting and not too handy with technical stuff. If that is the case, this overview will serve you well, though most podcasters who are technically challenged prefer to outsource their podcast production.

> "20% of adults report listening to podcasts at least occasionally. That is a lot of people you can reach with your voice! "
>
> — Flip This Risk® Books

Do not let this information intimidate you! Most people get started with their podcast with as little as a built-in smartphone microphone and random thoughts.

Anchor.fm is excellent for first-timers, and it is easy to use. As you "graduate" in the production area, you can hire someone else to do the heavy technical lifting.

So, here are a few things to know about what goes on behind the scenes. Be forewarned, it is technical!!!... but keep reading!

- A podcast generator maintains a central list of the files on a server as a web feed that one can access through the Internet. The listener or viewer uses special client application software on a computer or media player, known as a podcatcher, which accesses this web feed, checks it for updates, and downloads any new files in the series.
- This process can be automated to download new files automatically, so it may seem to listeners as though podcasters broadcast or "push" new episodes to them. Files are stored locally on the user›s device, ready for offline use.
- Several different mobile applications allow people to follow and listen to podcasts. Many of these applications allow users to download podcasts or stream them on demand. Most podcast players or

applications enable listeners to skip around the podcast and to control the playback speed.

- Podcasting has been considered a converged medium (a medium that brings together audio, the web, and portable media players) and a disruptive technology that has caused some individuals in radio broadcasting to reconsider established practices and preconceptions about audiences, consumption, production, and distribution.
- Podcasts can be produced at little to no cost and are usually disseminated free of charge, which sets this medium apart from the traditional 20th-Century model of "gate-kept" media and their production tools.
- Podcasters can, however, still monetize their podcasts by allowing companies to purchase ad time. They can also garner support from listeners through crowdfunding websites like Patreon, which provides special extras and content to listeners for a fee.

Podcasting is very much a horizontal media form—producers are consumers, consumers may become producers, and can engage in conversations with each other.

What Tools Do You Need?

For beginners, you need a quality microphone. Fortunately, a good microphone today is only around $50. The Snowball by Blue Microphones is the most popular. Do a little research and find a quality microphone. Remember that you are only recording your voice. You do not need a microphone that can handle the crushing volume of a drum set.

In a pinch, a combination headset-microphone can work well enough to get started. Move up to a better microphone when your finances allow. A headset combo is also a good option if you are interviewing others. Remember that you must hear the other person without the sound spilling over into your microphone. A computer to store the recordings. There are many alternatives to a computer, but you will need a computer to upload your podcast anyway.

That is all you need to get started. There's no excuse! A simple microphone and your computer are all you need to make a high-quality podcast. Start looking for a microphone today. You can get started on your first podcast immediately.

> **"As a podcaster, much like an entrepreneur, you need to have perseverance and resilience."**
>
> **— Mark Savant**

Creating your first podcast

- Choose a format. Go solo or have multiple guests. Most podcasters stick to a single structure and occasionally change it up. Your listeners will probably grow to like a particular format, but don't be afraid to make adjustments.
- Prepare. Unless you're very talented, you'll want notes, if not a full script. If you're interviewing someone, have questions ready.
- Consider the purpose of the podcast. What are you trying to share, teach, or explain? Perhaps your podcast is strictly for entertainment purposes.
- Record in a quiet space. People don't enjoy listening to background noise. It's distracting and shows a lack of professionalism.
- Edit appropriately. There are many audio programs available for cutting and pasting sections of your podcast. Many of them are free. Ensure that

any guests who participated in your podcast have the opportunity to review your edits before making the podcast public.

What could be easier? It can be a little more intimidating to put your voice online than writing a blog post. But that also makes it more effective. You're putting a part of yourself out there for the world to experience. Once you've recorded your podcast, it's time to make it available to others.

Getting Your Podcast to the Masses

You can send out your podcast in several ways:

Create an RSS feed. You can upload your podcast to a single site, and it will automatically be delivered to your subscribers. Use iTunes. iTunes will also provide your podcast to subscribers. People will also be able to search for it. You can choose whether or not to charge a fee.

After uploading to iTunes, you can expect it will take approximately 5-7 days until your podcast is available. There is a review process. Upload your podcast to other sites. Soundcloud is a popular platform and provides multiple sharing options. Use social media.

NOTES

4

Types of Podcasts

Here are a few examples and the popular audio podcast formats that may give you some fresh ideas.

Enhanced podcasts

An **enhanced podcast** or **slidecast** includes links to images synchronized with the podcast, turning it into a narrated slide show.

Scripted podcast

A **scripted podcast** (also referred to as a "fiction podcast" or "narrative podcast") is like a radio drama but in podcast form. They deliver a fictional story, usually told over multiple episodes and seasons, using numerous voice actors, dialogue, sound effects, and music to enrich the story.

> **"Podcasting is an amazing opportunity to exponentially reach your target audience."**
> **— Deb Coviello**

Scripted podcasts have attracted several well-known actors as voice talents, including Demi Moore, Matthew McConaughey, Kristen Wiig, and Rami Malek, as well as from content producers like Netflix, Spotify, Marvel, and DC Comics.

While science-fiction and horror are pretty famous, scripted podcasts cover a full range of literary genres from romance, comedy, and drama to fantasy, sci-fi, and detective fiction. Examples of scripted podcasts include *The Bright Sessions*, *Homecoming*, and *Wolverine: The Long Night*.

Podcast novels

A **podcast novel** (also known as a "serialized audiobook" or "podcast audiobook") is a literary form that combines the concepts of a podcast and an audiobook. Like a traditional novel, a podcast novel is a work of literary fiction; however, it is recorded into episodes delivered online over a period.

The episodes may be delivered automatically via RSS or through a website, blog, or other syndication methods. In addition, they can be released on a regular schedule, e.g., once a week, or irregularly as each episode is completed.

Similarly, as audiobooks, some podcast novels are elaborately narrated with sound effects and separate voice actors for each character, similar to a radio play or scripted podcast. Still, many have a single narrator and few or no sound effects.

Some podcast novelists give away a free podcast version of their book as a form of promotion. On occasion, such novelists have secured publishing contracts to have their novels printed.

Podcast novelists have commented that podcasting their novels lets them build audiences even if they cannot get a publisher to buy their books. These audiences then make it easier to secure a printing deal with a publisher later.

These podcast novelists also claim the exposure that releasing a free podcast gains them makes up because they are giving away their work for free.

Video podcasts

A **video podcast** or **vodcast** is a podcast that contains video content. Web television series are often distributed as video podcasts. *Dead End Days, a* serialized dark comedy about zombies released from October 31, 2003, through 2004, is commonly believed to be the first video podcast.

Live podcasts

Several podcasts are recorded either in total or for specific episodes in front of a live audience. Ticket sales allow the podcasters an additional way of monetizing. Some podcasts create specific live shows to tour, which are not necessarily included on the podcast feed. Events including the London Podcast Festival, SF Sketchfest, and others regularly give a platform for podcasters to perform live to audiences.

NOTES

5

Top Risks Every Podcaster Should Avoid

Risk is something that none of us can avoid. Yet, it is part of everything we do. Whether it is skydiving, investing in the stock market, winning the lottery, taking a risk, avoiding risk, or accepting risk is a decision that we make every day.

Should you take the train instead of driving the car to work to avoid the risk of being late? Should you purchase additional insurance during peak hurricane season? Should you start a business with the chance of gaining financial independence? All these questions require us to think about the risk of pursuing an opportunity or gaining a benefit.

Let us do a quick word association game.

When you think of the word **RISK**, what is the first thing that comes to mind?

What does RISK mean to you?

Risk is

I teach a course on risk management for industry professionals. Every time I invite them to complete this word association game, I get different answers.

They have said that **risk is a threat, impact, potential loss, a gamble, uncertainty.**

Frankly, it depends on who you ask!

The Merriam-Webster Dictionary defines **RISK** as the "possibility of loss or injury." But most of us do not wake up in the morning focusing on what we can lose. Instead, we rise with hope and expectation about what is possible! That is the frame of thought for this book.

In a nutshell, the positive things that we pursue involve some level of risk. The goal is to manage the risks to enjoy the benefits of the opportunities we seek.

The same goes for podcasts. It is without a doubt a great opportunity that offers a lot of perks-- like *increased credibility, influence, monetization, and exposure!* However, to continue to experience the benefits, we must manage those conditions that could block us from achieving our goal.

So, what are the top risks associated with podcasts that you should keep in mind as you pursue this opportunity?

We interviewed a few expert podcasters who offered up their opinions about the risk, opportunities, and challenges podcasters should be mindful of to achieve long-term success.

NOTES

Interview with Corey Poirier

FLIP THIS RISK® BOOKS: From your perspective, what are the top opportunities facing podcasters?

COREY: I feel podcasters have an opportunity to reach new people and turn them onto podcasts, creating long-term raving fans. Most people still have not heard a podcast, and it still has experienced so much growth that speaks for the long-term potential for all involved.

Podcasters can also build an intimate relationship with their listeners to leverage and grow their business (whether their business is the podcast itself or something related). Podcasters also can create new customers while also transforming the lives of those same customers in a way not before possible in the same way.

FLIP THIS RISK® BOOKS: What are the top risks/challenges podcasters face?

COREY: Because podcasting is on such a growth pattern, the most significant risk people face is using their time for podcasting instead of something else - only to give up before they experience the growth that is possible for those who stay the course. The risk is simply committing their time to a podcast rather than something else that could give them a more significant return if they stayed with it vs. giving up on podcasting too soon.

FLIP THIS RISK® BOOKS: What can podcasters do to address these risks?

COREY: Realize that the rewards inolve sticking around and that 100 of the right listeners is as big a thing as 1 million of the wrong listeners. So really, what podcasters can do is figure out who THEIR people are and aim to serve those people and realize that you only need a small number of raving fans to impact and transform lives and even build a business around the podcast.

Corey Poirier (aka. That Speaker Guy) is a Multiple-Time TEDx Speaker, bLU Talks Founder Featured in and seen on NBC, ABC, Fox, TEDx, Entrepreneur on Fire, Entrepreneur Magazine, Second City, The CW, and CBS

NOTES

Interview with Meiko S. Patton

FLIP THIS RISK® BOOKS: From your perspective, what are the top opportunities facing podcasters?

MEIKO: With a plethora of podcasts, the top priority facing podcasters is visibility. Without being seen, it is impossible to be heard. I believe podcasters need to jump on a platform like Clubhouse and listen to how real podcasters are getting noticed. I host a weekly Clubhouse room all about podcast marketing. I give tips to help podcasters promote their podcast.

FLIP THIS RISK® BOOKS: What are the top risks/challenges podcasters face?

MEIKO: In my opinion, it is a risk if podcasters do not take advantage of the free knowledge available in Clubhouse. Business owners spend up to 70 hours a week and give away free information to help podcasters. If podcasters are not in those rooms getting that free mentorship, it can be detrimental to their business.

FLIP THIS RISK® BOOKS: What can podcasters do to address these risks?

MEIKO: Podcasters can change the odds and put them in their favor by giving back. When you go into a clubhouse room, podcasters can listen, but they can also give back in the form of their knowledge and skill.

There might be someone doing what you are doing, but no one can do it the way you do it because of your life experience.

Focus on giving, and you will receive in return. That equation will always lower your risks.

Meiko S. Patton is a Clubhouse Strategic Communications Consultant. She is the author of the Amazon best-selling book "A Postage Stamp Saved My Life."

NOTES

Interview with Karen Hardy

FLIP THIS RISK® BOOKS: From your perspective, what are the top opportunities facing podcasters?

KAREN: Podcasting allows expanding a brand and reaching a potential stream of clients not accessible through other social media platforms. Podcasting also serves as an additional venue for communicating a brand message while also serving others, which is a powerful combination for expanding recognition of who you are and what you can do to help others.

FLIP THIS RISK® BOOKS: What are the top risks/challenges podcasters face?

KAREN: One of the most significant risks for podcasters is not integrating the medium into their overall business strategy.

If it is not a hobby, podcasters need to be specific about why this platform is a positive addition to its value chain because of the amount of time invested in making it a good product for consumption.

Secondly, tactically speaking, inconsistency is a significant risk that will lead to the creator's abandonment before the benefits can be fully realized.

FLIP THIS RISK® BOOKS: What can podcasters do to address these risks?

KAREN: Podcasters should decide and map out early on what the strategic value is of adding a podcast to its business model --- not because it is popular, but because it will eventually lead to more sales or new clients.

Karen Hardy runs a successful risk management consulting firm. She is also the creator and host of Flip This Risk® Podcast. It reaches audiences in 12 countries and is listed as a *"Top 50 Podcast to Listen to"* by Thinkers360. You can access the podcast on all podcast platforms, including Alexa, Apple, Google Podcast, ListenNotes, and Amazon Music. Subscribe to our podcast NOW at FlipThisRiskPodcast.com

NOTES

Interview with Sarah Barnes-Humphrey

FLIP THIS RISK® BOOKS: From your perspective, what are the top opportunities facing podcasters?

SARAH: There are so many! Not only is it a great way to create content and get involved in the community, but you can also take your expertise and create a unique, fun, and profitable business for yourself while helping to connect people.

FLIP THIS RISK® BOOKS: What are the top risks/challenges podcasters face?

SARAH: There is a lot of content out there for people to consume, so how will you be different? How will you position yourself to be the resource of choice?

Other challenges are:

- Getting Started
- Coordinating the interviews
- Staying on track with publishing, being consistent
- Reaching new listeners
- Coming up with fresh content
- Staying up to date with trends
- Monetizing

FLIP THIS RISK® BOOKS: What can podcasters do to address these risks?

SARAH: Patience and consistency are vital to building something great that people can rely on and trust. Having the mantra of progress over perfection will help you get started. Using tools like Calendly will help coordinate schedules. Use and understand social platforms to help reach new audiences.

Monetizing is the biggest challenge podcasters have. It is something I have tested and succeeded at, so I have taken the formula for my business at Let us Talk Supply Chain and offering a course on how to build and monetize your podcast. You can sign up for the pilot program here: https://expertsonair.fm/podcast-for-profit/

Sarah Barnes-Humphrey is a supply chain leader. She is the founder of Let us Talk Supply Chain (Digital Media) and Co-Founder of Shipz.com

NOTES

Interview with Deb Coviello

FLIP THIS RISK® BOOKS: From your perspective, what are the top opportunities facing podcasters?

DEB: Podcasting is a fantastic opportunity to reach your target audience and build your brand impact exponentially. I also leverage the power of creating intimate conversations with my guests to build trust and open the dialogue for collaboration that supports both our businesses.

FLIP THIS RISK® BOOKS: What are the top risks/challenges podcasters face?

DEB: The time it takes to vet the ideal guest and the business processes to provide an excellent guest/listener experience is challenging. To do it well and make it memorable takes a lot of time for the podcaster.

We want to be connected to build long-term relationships, but the administrative part requires podcast management resources that the entrepreneur might not have.

FLIP THIS RISK® BOOKS: What can podcasters do to address these risks?

DEB: I need a strategy for sponsors or monetization to return the income to the business, further building out the media platform. It is a lot of work to figure out how to monetize quickly.

Deb Coviello is Host of The Drop-in CEO™, a Top 50 Podcast to listen to by Thinkers360.

NOTES

Interview with Mark Savant

FLIP THIS RISK® BOOKS: From your perspective, what are the top opportunities facing podcasters?

MARK: The most significant opportunity is in nurturing relationships and opening doors. When done thoughtfully and strategically, podcasting will allow you to speak with people you usually would not. It will open doors to stages and businesses you usually would not be able to access.

FLIP THIS RISK® BOOKS: What are the top risks/challenges podcasters face?

MARK: The most significant challenge podcasters face is burnout. It is common to overestimate what you can accomplish. Many podcasters take on too much and do not make it past seven episodes. Going into a podcast with the proper guidance, plan, and processes dramatically improve the chances of success.

FLIP THIS RISK® BOOKS: What can podcasters do to address these risks?

MARK: As a podcaster, much like an entrepreneur, you need to have perseverance and resilience. These characteristics are difficult to teach, BUT if you surround yourself with the right people, it helps dramatically. From working with a coach that can help put the systems in place, joining a group of podcasters also hungry for success, to surrounding yourself with the right people—all of this is enormous.

Mark Savant is the founder of Mark Savant Media at **www.marksavantmedia.com**

His podcast is a top-rated podcast for entrepreneurs.

NOTES

6

Managing Your Success for Podcasting

In the previous chapter, we shared insights from successful podcasters regarding their thoughts on the risk and opportunities of podcasting.

But why should risk be a part of the podcast conversation? First, consider that the most successful leaders of organizations and entrepreneurs practice good risk management.

Take, for example, Jeff Hoffman. Jeff is super successful and is the founding executive of Priceline.com. When Jeff was interviewed on the Flip This Risk® Podcast, he clearly expressed his risk management practice when it came to achieving his goals. Here are his thoughts:

> **"So here is something I learned over time. For most people, risk equals the unknown. It is the fear of the unknown that people are afraid of. They ask, "what if this doesn't work? What will happen to me?" I developed a technique that works for me that really helps me with risk now. And here is what I do: I sit down and do this risk analysis. I mentally and emotionally put myself in the worst "what if" scenario... as if I am living it. But if you leave it as an unknown, its super crazy."**
>
> **— Jeff Hoffman**

To summarize Jeff's point, it is best to know what things can trip you up from achieving your success than to avoid knowing what those things are.

That is the benefit of the **H.O.W. Model™**.

The **H.O.W. Model™** (cleverly named for simplicity, of course!) is the acronym for the Hardy Opportunity

Window™ Model. It is a framework, a technique like Jeff used to assess risk in his personal life. And, as a consultant, it reflects the approach I use to advise national and international organizations.

The model is a simplified version of international standards and concepts used by some of the most successful companies like Amazon, Google, Netflix, Disney, Costco, and Lowes.

These companies understand that you cannot achieve greatness without managing risk!

We all encounter "windows" of opportunity, but this skill set should not and is not reserved for just the big, successful companies.

Think about it.

If Jeff Hoffman, a multi-millionaire and astounding entrepreneur, uses a technique for sizing up his opportunities by analyzing his risks, shouldn't you?

NOTES

7

Using the H.O.W. Model™

Hardy Opportunity Window™
© 2021 Karen Hardy

Our expert podcasters identified specific risks and challenges that can keep you from achieving podcast success in the preceding chapters.

These are by no means all the risks you will face, but gives you a sense of the immediate dangers to pay attention to:

1. negative trade-offs of time
2. inconsistency
3. a lack of a strategy
4. missing out on free mentorship
5. podcast fade/burnout

Now that we know what our risks are let us practice some fundamental risk management techniques!

3- Easy Steps

Step 1: The first step is to review the H.O.W. Model™.

The framework provides a summary of the five phases of opportunity management:

1. Organize
2. Identify
3. Assess
4. Respond
5. Check-in/Reset

As you pursue opportunities, take time to walk through each of the five phases to help trigger your thoughts and navigate your path to success.

Step 2: Determine the importance of each risk.

Revisiting the risk and challenges that our experts identified, in the "Rating" column, enter **H** for High, **M** for Medium, or **L** for Low

Legend

- **(H)** High risk means = it will wipe you out/sideline you
- **(M)** Medium risk means = it will be challenging, but you have resources to adjust
- **(L)** Low risk means = it is not an immediate threat to your success

Rate your Risks!

The Risk	**Rating**
Negative trade-offs	
Inconsistency	
A lack of strategy	
Missing out on free mentorship	
Podcast fade/burnout	

Step 3: Act! What actions can you take to avoid these risks?

The Risk	**Actions to take**
Negative trade-offs	
Inconsistency	
A lack of strategy	
Missing out on free mentorship	
Podcast fade/burnout	

By following the **H.O.W. Model™**, you have a better chance to act with confidence, rather than being paralyzed by the constant fear of the unknown.

The H.O.W. Model™

Hardy Opportunity Window™/ © 2021 Karen Hardy
Framing Opportunities within the Context of Risk-Taking™

	**Organize** your thoughts. Think about the goals and objectives of your opportunity. Think about the direction in which you are headed, what you want to achieve, the resources needed to get there, and any essential timelines and milestones worth tracking.
	**Identify** the risks to your objectives. What can hamper your progress towards success? Brainstorm and write down multiple "what if" scenarios. Then, place yourself emotionally in those situations and think about the outcome of each situation.
	**Assess** whether the outcome and impact of each scenario is something that you can live with (accept) as is, avoid, or do something about (mitigate). Ask yourself: Does the opportunity outweigh the worst scenario, or does the worst scenario outweigh the opportunity in terms of benefits and rewards?

	**Respond** to the situation with confidence, knowing that you have already thought through the scenario. Adjust. Establish and strengthen resilience skills. Seek assistance. What reinforcements do you need for future and continued success?
	**Check-in** frequently to revisit your opportunities, including the original goals and objectives.

Remember, it is best to know what risk you will face in pursuing your opportunity (such as podcasting) than wonder about and fear the unknown. Of course, things can change over time, and adjustments may be needed, but at least by completing each of these steps, you have a better sense of what challenges to expect for achievement and improve your chances of success!

NOTES

8

Legal Talking Points for Podcasters

Some experienced podcasters have noted that they require their guests to sign a podcasting agreement. This requirement may or may not be necessary for others.

However, since some are practicing this, you may want to seek legal guidance from a professional in the field of entertainment law or intellectual property law to see if it is a good or idea.

For those interested and involved in podcasting, this list of podcasting talking points can be used to jumpstart general ideas about the type of topics you may want to discuss with a legal professional.

> **"Business owners are literally spending up to 70 hours a week and more giving away free information to help podcasters."**
>
> **— Meiko S. Patton**

This checklist should only be used as a starting point. It is not considered to be legal advice.

You may find that you do not need any legal advice in creating and producing your podcast, but it never hurts to do an informal check-in, especially if you are thinking of growing your podcast.

Potential Legal Talking Points Checklist	
	Using written content created by someone else
	Instances where copyright permission is not required
	Using a fact, an idea, a theory, or slogan
	Using works that are in the public domain
	Using US Government work
	Using your written consent

	Incorporating pre-existing audio voice recordings
	Interviewing someone or asking someone to join you in conversation as part of your podcast
	Using Music
	Licenses you will need
	Using videos/images

Source: Portions adapted from "Podcasting Legal Guide http://wiki.creativecommons.org/Podcasting_Legal_Guide © 2006 Colette Vogele of Vogele & Associates, Mia Garlick of Creative Commons and Berkman Center Clinical Program in Cyberlaw. This Guide was produced as part of the Non-Residential Fellowship Program of the Center for Internet & Society at Stanford Law School."

NOTES

Podcasting Resources

Acast.com- A curated, fully integrated podcast marketplace.

Bonjoror.com- Convert, retain, and grow your customers with personal video messages.

Castro.fm- It makes it easy to manage lots of podcasts and enjoy the best episodes of all your favorite shows.

Clipscribe.com- Easily create attention-commanding subtitles for your videos for social media.

GetPodTube.net- Publish your YouTube videos as a podcast.

Headliner.app - Create videos to promote your podcast, radio show, or blog.

ListenNotes.com- A comprehensive podcast database online. Discover best podcasts. Search podcast show notes and audio transcripts.

Overcast.fm- Works with the open, standard world of podcasts. There are no terms to agree to, no rights to give up, and no loss of control over your podcast or its distribution.

PodfestExpo.com- A community of people interested in and passionate about sharing their voice and message with the world through the powerful mediums of audio and video.

Podmatch.com- Automatically matches ideal podcast hosts and guests for interviews.

Podpage.com- Automatically create a podcast website in 5 minutes.

Riverside.fm- Record podcasts and video interviews in studio quality from anywhere. All from the browser.

Simplecast.com- A framework built for audio. An audio streaming infrastructure delivering millions of minutes of audio content every single day.

Snip-It App- Use it to snip something off your phone/ tab screen and sharing it with someone. An alternative to taking screenshots.

StreamYard.com- A live streaming studio in your browser.

Wavve.co- Turn your podcast or musical audio into engaging animated videos to share on social media.

Zubtitle.com- Automatically generate captions for your videos.

Additional Resources

For training courses on risk management:
www.FlipThisRiskAcademy.com

Subscribe to the Flip This Risk® Podcast at
FlipThisRiskPodcast.com

Watch Flip This Risk® on YouTube:
bit.ly/FlipThisRiskTVChannel

Receive Free Risk Strategy Videos:
bit.ly/DrHardyStrategyVideos

Follow Dr. Karen Hardy on LinkedIn:
www.linkedin.com/in/drkarenhardyspeaks

Invite Dr. Hardy to speak at your event:
www.drkarenhardyspeaks.com

Notes (Chapters 1-4, 8)

1. "Podcast Production". *Harvard Graduate School of Education. 2012. Archived from the original on July 10, 2012. Retrieved July 10, 2012. This code enables specially designed software to locate and track new versions or episodes of a particular podcast ...*

2. ^ *Berry, Richard (2015). "Serial and Ten Years of Podcasting: Has the Medium Grown up?". Radio, Sounds & Internet: 299–209. Archived from the original on July 4, 2020. Retrieved July 4, 2020 – via Academia.edu.*

3. ^ Jump up to:a b *Berry, Richard (May 1, 2006). "Will the iPod Kill the Radio Star? Profiling Podcasting as Radio" (PDF). Convergence.* ***12****(2): 143–162. doi:10.1177/1354856506066522. S2CID 111593307. Archived (PDF) from the original on February 26, 2020. Retrieved July 4, 2020.*

4. ^ *Stratmann, Jo (July 20, 2011). "'Horizontal Media' - How Social Media Has Changed Journalism". FreshMinds. Archived from the original on November 16, 2017. Retrieved November 15, 2017.*

5. ^ *"Definition of Podcast in English". OxfordDictionaries.com. Archived from the original on May 28, 2019. Retrieved November 15, 2017.*

6. ^ *Hammersley, Ben (February 12, 2004). "Why Online Radio Is Booming". The Guardian. Archived from the original on June 21, 2020. Retrieved November 16, 2017.*

7. ^ *Sawyer, Miranda (November 20, 2015). "The Man Who Accidentally Invented the Word 'Podcast'" (MP3). BBC Radio 4. Archived from the original on April 2, 2019. Retrieved November 15, 2017.*

8. ^ *Gregoire, Danny (September 12, 2004). "How to Handle Getting Past Episodes?". Yahoo Groups. Archived from the original on April 13, 2013. Retrieved July 4, 2020.*

9. ^ *Owens, Simon (February 6, 2015). "Slate's Podcast Audience Has Tripled in a Year, and It's Bet on Audio Over Video Continues to Pay Off". Nieman Lab. Archived from the original on December 6, 2020. Retrieved December 6, 2020.*

10. ^ *Levy, Steven (October 23, 2006). The Perfect Thing: How the iPod Shuffles Commerce, Culture, and Coolness. Simon & Schuster. p. 239. ISBN 978-0-7432-8522-3. Archived from the original on July 4, 2020. Retrieved July 4, 2020.*

11. ^ *"Apple Brings Podcasts Into iTunes". BBC News. June 28, 2005. Archived from the original on December 14, 2019. Retrieved November 15, 2017.*

12. ^ *"FAQ - The Official TWiT Wiki". TWiT.tv. January 9, 2009. Archived from the original on January 20, 2019. Retrieved November 15, 2017.*

13. ^ *Ricks, Byron (2007). "Create your own podcast: What you need to know to be a podcaster". Microsoft Windows. Archived from the original on December 25, 2015. Retrieved July 15, 2020.*

14. ^ *"Follow our podcast': Apple Podcasts to stop using 'subscribe'". podnews.net. 2021-03-09. Retrieved 2021-03-12.*

15. ^ *Louis, Tristan (October 13, 2000). "Suggestion for RSS 0.92 Specification". groups.yahoo.com. Archived from the original on November 22, 2016. Retrieved July 24, 2020.*

16. ^ *Pot, Justin (August 24, 2013). "The Evolution of the Podcast -- How a Medium Was Born [Geek History]". MakeUseOf. Archived from the original on December 6, 2020. Retrieved December 6, 2020.*

17. ^ *Massing, Michael (April 2, 2019). "Are the Humanities History?". The New York Review of Books. Archived from the original on August 6, 2020. Retrieved April 12, 2019.*

18. ^ *"Podcast". redOrbit. March 16, 2013. Archived from the original on June 30, 2013. Retrieved December 6, 2020.*

19. ^ Jump up to:[a] [b] *Watson, Stephanie (March 26, 2005). "How Podcasting Works § Podcasting History". HowStuffWorks. Archived from the original on July 16, 2020. Retrieved November 15, 2017.*

20. ^ *Schichter, Matt (September 12, 2014). "Matt Schichter Interviews by Scared Goose Productions on Apple Podcasts". Apple Podcasts. Archived from the original on March 11, 2018. Retrieved March 11, 2018.*

21. ^ *Geoghegan, Michael W.; Klass, Dan (November 4, 2007). Podcast Solutions: The Complete Guide to Audio and Video Podcasting (2nd ed.). New York: Apress. p. 4. ISBN 978-1-59059-905-1. Archived from the original on August 20, 2020. Retrieved November 15, 2017.*

22. ^ *Benson, Richard (November 14, 2019). "An Aural History of the Podcast: The History of the Podcast (By Those Who Helped*

Make Them a Thing)". Esquire Middle East. Retrieved December 6,2020.

23. ^ *Ciccarelli, Stephanie (April 4, 2015). "The Origins of Podcasting". Voices.com. Archived from the original on April 25, 2019. Retrieved November 15, 2017.*

24. ^ *Blass, Evan (September 24, 2006). "With "Pod" on Lockdown, Apple Goes After "Podcast"". Engadget. Archived from the original on February 4, 2019. Retrieved November 15, 2017.*

25. ^ *Gerry Smith (February 22, 2019). "Everybody Makes Podcasts. Can Anyone Make Them Profitable?". Bloomberg Businessweek. Bloomberg L.P. Archived from the original on October 22, 2019. Retrieved December 20 2019.*

26. ^ *Staff (April 5 2019). "The Podcast Consumer 2019". edisonresearch.com. Edison Research. p. 8. Archived from the original (PDF) on November 26 2019. Retrieved 20 December2019.*

27. ^ *Sawyer, Miranda (2020-05-03). "It's boom time for podcasts – but will going mainstream kill the magic?". The Observer. ISSN 0029-7712. Retrieved 2020-05-03.*

28. ^ *Smith, Steve (November 22, 2016). "Podcasts: Can They Hear Us Now". EContent. Vol. 39 no. 8. Information Today, Inc. p. 9. Archived from the original on July 16, 2019. Retrieved November 15, 2017.*

29. ^ *"Podcast Trademark Rejection Documents". USPTO. Retrieved November 15, 2017.*

30. ^ *"List of US Podcast Trademarks". USPTO. Retrieved November 15, 2017.*

31. ^ *Holliman, Russell (September 26, 2006). "Podcast Ready Receives Cease & Desist from Apple Computer". Podcast Ready. Archived from the original on October 5, 2006. Retrieved December 7, 2020.*

32. ^ *Heater, Brian (March 24, 2009). "Apple's Legal Team Going After 'Pod' People". PC Magazine. Archived from the original on April 2, 2019. Retrieved November 15, 2017.*

33. ^ *Longo, Jeffrey (September 25, 2006). "Podcast Trademark Controversy". MacRumors. Archived from the original on August 6, 2020. Retrieved November 15, 2017.*

34. ^ *"Copy of the Letter from Apple Trademark Department". Flickr. Global Geek Podcast. November 16, 2006. Archived from the original on August 6, 2020. Retrieved November 15,2017.*

35. ^ Jump up to: [a] [b] *Nazer, Daniel (May 30, 2013). "Help Save Podcasting!". EFF. Archived from the original on November 11, 2020. Retrieved November 15, 2017.*

36. ^ *"System for Disseminating Media Content Representing Episodes in a Serialized Sequence". Google Patents. October 2, 1996. Archived from the original on November 12, 2020. Retrieved November 15, 2017.*

37. ^ *Samuels, Julie (February 5, 2013). "Podcasting Community Faces Patent Troll Threat; EFF Wants to Help". EFF. Archived from the original on November 12, 2020. Retrieved November 15, 2017. Personal Audio is claiming that it owns a patent that covers podcasting technology.*

38. ^ *"EFF v. Personal Audio LLC". EFF. April 21, 2014. Archived from the original on August 6, 2020. Retrieved November 15,2017.*

39. ^ *Nazeer, Daniel (August 18, 2014). "The Good, the Bad, and the Ugly of Adam Carolla's Settlement with the Podcasting Troll". EFF. Archived from the original on November 12, 2020. Retrieved November 15, 2017.*

40. ^ *Fung, Brian (April 10, 2015). "How the Government Just Protected Some of Your Favorite Podcasts". The Washington Post. Archived from the original on November 3, 2019. Retrieved November 15, 2017.*

41. ^ *"Definition of enhanced podcast". PCMAG. Ziff Davis. Archived from the original on October 22, 2020. Retrieved February 26, 2020.*

42. ^ *Skinner, Oliver (July 30, 2020). "Fiction Podcasts: The Medium Giving Rise to a New Generation of Audio Storytellers". Voices.com. Retrieved January 20, 2021.*

43. ^ *Kornelis, Chris (December 25, 2020). "From Demi Moore to Matthew McConaughey, Screen Stars Are Turning to Podcasts". The Wall Street Journal. Retrieved January 19,2021.*

44. ^ *"Netflix Creates Its First Scripted Podcast, As An Extension To TV Show". Inside Radio. November 1, 2019. Retrieved January 20, 2021.*

45. ^ *White, Jordan (May 30, 2018). "Wolverine: The Long Night opens up the possibilities for a Marvel Podcast Universe". The Verge. Retrieved January 20, 2021.*

46. ^ *Jennings, Collier (July 18, 2020). "DC, Spotify Cut Deal for Multiple Scripted Podcast Series". CBR.com.*

47. ^ *Florin, Hector (January 31, 2009). "Podcasting Your Novel: Publishing's Next Wave?". Time. Archived from the original on August 6, 2020. Retrieved November 15, 2017.*

48. ^ *Cadelago, Chris (April 5, 2008). "Take My Book. It's Free". San Francisco Chronicle. Archived from the original on October 22, 2020. Retrieved November 15, 2017.*

49. ^ *Newman, Andrew Adam (March 1, 2007). "Authors Find Their Voice, and Audience, in Podcasts". The New York Times. Archived from the original on November 23, 2020. Retrieved November 15, 2017.*

50. ^ *Gaughran, David (September 5, 2011). ""Free" Really Can Make You Money – A Dialogue with Moses Siregar III". Let us Get Digital. Archived from the original on October 14, 2011. Retrieved November 15, 2017.*

51. ^ *Ellis, Jessica (2008). "What is a Video Podcast?". Wise Geek. Archived from the original on August 9, 2020. Retrieved November 15, 2017.*

52. ^ *Arboine, Niellah (August 21, 2019). "How to Get 20% off Tickets to the London Podcast Festival". Bustle. Archived from the original on August 6, 2020. Retrieved March 9, 2020.*

53. ^ *"SF Sketchfest Announces Additions to Festival Lineup". Broadway World. December 6, 2019. Archived from the original on November 17, 2020. Retrieved March 9, 2020*

About The Author

Dr. Karen Hardy is a two-time bestselling author and recipient of the Most Promising New Textbook Award. She was inducted into the National Academy of Best-Selling Authors. Her book on risk management reached #6 on the Amazon Top 100 List for Risk Management.

Dr. Hardy's career includes experience at the White House Office of Management and Budget, Executive Office of the U.S. President, and building an enterprise risk management function at a $7B public sector agency.

She is the co-author of *Mastering the Art of Success* with Jack Canfield (creator of *Chicken Soup for the Soul*) and co-producer of the four-time Emmy Award-winning documentary film, *A New Leash on Life: The K9s for Warriors* Story, a movie about the risks of veterans with PTSD. The film can be seen on Amazon Prime and PBS stations.

She is the founder and creator of the Flip This Risk® brand.

Other Titles
that May be of Interest to You

Made in the USA
Monee, IL
04 November 2026

67380052R00056